W9-APX-840

Masters of Music
THE WORLD'S GREATEST COMPOSERS

The Life and Times of

Gilbert and Sullivan

P.O. Box 196
Hockessin, Delaware 19707

Masters of Music
THE WORLD'S GREATEST COMPOSERS

Titles in the Series

The Life and Times of...

Johann Sebastian Bach

Ludwig van Beethoven

Irving Berlin

Hector Berlioz

Leonard Bernstein

Johannes Brahms

Frederic Chopin

Duke Ellington

Stephen Foster

George Gershwin

William Gilbert and Arthur Sullivan

George Frideric Handel

Franz Joseph Haydn

Scott Joplin

Franz Liszt

Felix Mendelssohn

Wolfgang Amadeus Mozart

Franz Peter Schubert

John Philip Sousa

Igor Stravinsky

Peter Ilyich Tchaikovsky

Giuseppe Verdi

Antonio Lucio Vivaldi

Richard Wagner

Visit us on the web: www.mitchelllane.com

Comments? email us: mitchelllane@mitchelllane.com

Masters of Music
THE WORLD'S GREATEST COMPOSERS

The Life and Times of

Gilbert and Sullivan

by Jim Whiting

Printing   1   2   3   4   5   6   7   8
     Library of Congress Cataloging-in-Publication Data
Whiting, Jim, 1943-
          The life and times of Gilbert and Sullivan/Jim Whiting.
              p. cm. — (Masters of music)
     Includes bibliographical references and index.
          ISBN 1-58415-276-1 (library bound)
     1. Sullivan, Arthur, Sir, 1842-1900—Juvenile Literature 2. Gilbert, W. S. (William Schwenck), 1836-1911—Juvenile literature. 3. Composers—England—Biography—Juvenile literature. 4. Librettists—England—Biography—Juvenile Literature. I. Title. II. Masters of music (Mitchell Lane Publishers)
ML3930.S95W45 2004
782.1'2'0922—DC22

                                                            2004020949

ABOUT THE AUTHOR: Jim Whiting has been a journalist, writer, editor, and photographer for more than 20 years. In addition to a lengthy stint as publisher of *Northwest Runner* magazine, Mr. Whiting has contributed articles to the *Seattle Times*, *Conde Nast Traveler*, *Newsday*, and *Saturday Evening Post*. He has written and edited more than 100 Mitchell Lane titles. His love of music inspired him to write this book. He lives in Washington state with his wife and two teenage sons.

PUBLISHER'S NOTE: This story is based on the author's extensive research, which he believes to be accurate. Documentation of such research is contained on page 46.

The internet sites referenced herein were active as of the publication date. Due to the fleeting nature of some web sites, we cannot guarantee they will all be active when you are reading this book.

Contents

The Life and Times of

Gilbert and Sullivan

by Jim Whiting

Chapter 1
Pirates and Pinafores 7
FYInfo*: The Royal Navy 11

Chapter 2
A Failed Lawyer, a Successful Writer 13
FYInfo: Arthur Conan Doyle 17

Chapter 3
A Brilliant Young Composer 19
FYInfo: The World's Biggest Ship 23

Chapter 4
A Fateful Meeting 25
FYInfo: Richard D'Oyly Carte 31

Chapter 5
Cracks in the Foundation 33
FYInfo: Setting Standards 37

Chapter 6
The End of the Music 39
FYInfo: Rodgers and Hammerstein 42

Chronology 43
Timeline in History 44
Chapter Notes 45
Further Reading 46
Works Consulted 46
Glossary 47
Selected Works 47
Index 48
* For Your Information

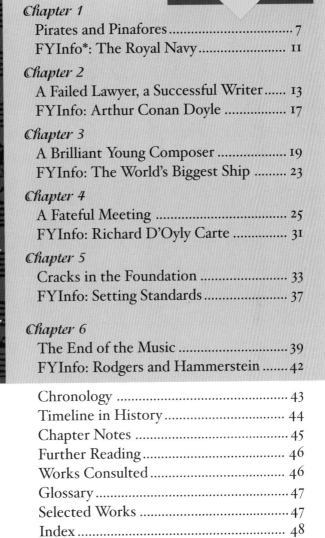

This is the title page of the original sheet music from the Gilbert and Sullivan operetta The Pirates of Penzance. One of their most popular works, Pirates is often performed by high school drama groups. It includes the tune to "Hail, hail, the gang's all here!"

CHAPTER

I

Pirates and Pinafores

Soon after it began operating in 1999, Napster became the hottest name in music. It was a computer program that allowed its users to download music—even whole albums—from the Internet. There were several reasons for Napster's popularity. It was easy to use. It offered a staggering variety of music from which to choose. And it was free. With the cost of compact discs approaching twenty dollars, that was probably its main attraction.

Not everyone was happy with Napster. Recording artists and music companies opposed it. They claimed that it was cutting into sales and violating copyright laws. Some of them called Napster officials "thieves" and "pirates" and wanted to throw them into prison.

This wasn't the first time that pirates in music was an issue. More than a century ago, in 1879, a highly successful London light opera, or operetta, called *H.M.S. Pinafore,* came to the United States. It was the first major success for the two men who collaborated on it. William S. Gilbert wrote the operetta's libretto, or its words, and Arthur Sullivan composed the music.

H.M.S. stands for "Her {or His} Majesty's Ship." Like *USS* (for "United States Ship") before the name of an American vessel, the abbreviation was the mark of a warship in the Royal Navy. Many Royal Navy ships bore bold names such as *Conqueror, Courageous, Thunderer,* and *Victory.* Others were named after legendary warriors, such as *Achilles, Agamemnon,* and *Hercules.*

But a pinafore is a sleeveless garment similar to an apron, usually worn by little girls over a dress. It's hardly a name that would inspire its crew members to feats of glory. So the title of the play suggested that it was a comedy. People came to the theater expecting to laugh. Humor wasn't the only reason for *Pinafore*'s popularity. Its songs had tuneful melodies. Many of them became popular from the moment audiences first heard them.

American travelers who had seen the show in London, where it opened the previous summer, brought back enthusiastic reports. Word quickly spread throughout the country. As a result, *H.M.S. Pinafore* inspired the same sort of preopening buzz as blockbuster films such as *Harry Potter* and *Lord of the Rings* do today. (At that time, of course, there were no multiplex movie theaters.) There were many people who wanted to see the show when it opened early in 1879.

As David Eden explains, "It created a sensation comparable only to the Beatles craze of more recent memory. At one time it was played in nine theatres in New York simultaneously, and in forty-two throughout the country, besides uncounted touring companies. John Philip Sousa met his wife in one such company.

The impetus thus given to operatic performance laid the foundation of the American musical theatre."[1]

Music writer Harold Schonberg comments, "In Chicago, eleven companies staged *Pinafore* in 1879, some of them simultaneously. There were performances of *Pinafore* with all-black casts and, for the German-speaking population in America, *Pinafore* in German. . . . Some hundred-thousand barrel organs were built to play *Pinafore* selections."[2]

According to a contemporary report in *Dwight's Journal of Music,* "Hundreds of companies, professional and amateur, have been acting and singing it. In the great cities, *Pinafore* has held the stage in half a dozen theaters at once. . . . It has been served up in every theater and hall; church choirs go around the country singing it; every child sings and hums it; the tuneful images repeat themselves as in a multiplying mirror, from every wall, through every street and valley."[3]

Today, such an astounding success would mean millions of dollars in royalties. Then it was a very different story.

"Neither Gilbert nor Sullivan could draw a cent from these productions," according to writer Arthur Jacobs. "Under United States law, it was generally understood that the publication of a theatrical work made it public property, freely usable. The free-enterprise American promoters of *Pinafore* were exercising their rights—as London theatrical managers had put on French plays in translation without paying their authors. The promoters were infringing no law, no international convention (there were no international conventions on copyright in those days). It is usual to refer to them as pirates but they were not so in any strict sense."[4]

Near the end of 1879, Gilbert and Sullivan sailed for New York, where they were given star treatment. They had more on their minds than basking in the spotlight. They wanted to cash in on their overwhelming success. They mounted a "copyright performance" to establish their ownership of *H.M.S. Pinafore.* That meant that from then on, they would be entitled to royalties from *Pinafore* performances in the United States.

The two men probably realized that their "copyright performance" was too little, too late. The show was already so well established that it would be hard to stop every performance. Another reason for their coming to New York may have been that they had learned their lessons about copyright. They decided that their next operetta would open on December 30 in England and the following day in New York. That way they would have simultaneous copyrights in both countries. In view of what had happened with *Pinafore,* the title of that next operetta seemed especially appropriate.

It was *The Pirates of Penzance.* ◆

The Royal Navy

Admiral Nelson

During the Victorian era, "The sun never sets on the British Empire" was a popular saying. British colonies and dominions spanned virtually the entire globe. The primary reason Great Britain was so powerful and could control so much land was that the Royal Navy had control of the millions of square miles of ocean that linked its empire.

The Royal Navy had a proud history that dated back more than a millennium. One highlight was its resistance when the Spanish Armada tried to invade England in 1588. The smaller and more maneuverable English ships kept the Spanish from being able to come ashore and land their troops. Eventually the Armada was forced to sail around the northern tip of England, where many of its ships were destroyed by storms.

In the early days of the 19th century, the ships of the Royal Navy were the main reason that the French Emperor Napoléon couldn't invade England. Under the leadership of Admiral Horatio Nelson, the British destroyed a combined French and Spanish fleet at the battle of Trafalgar in 1805. Nelson's flagship, *Victory,* is still preserved as a monument to that triumph. Trafalgar Square—and its immense statue of Nelson—is a major London landmark.

By the time of Gilbert and Sullivan, the wooden sailing vessels that ruled the seas for centuries had given way to steam-powered iron ships. But the proud heritage of the Royal Navy was still strong. People believed that English sailors were better than any others— well trained, highly disciplined, and very courageous. While *H.M.S. Pinafore* pokes fun at many aspects of British life, the Royal Navy isn't one of them. Midway through the first act, a chorus sings, "A British tar [sailor] is a soaring soul,/As free as a mountain bird,/His energetic fist should be ready to resist/A dictatorial word."[5] Everyone in the audience would have agreed.

This photo of William Gilbert was probably taken in the mid-1870s, at about the time he began collaborating with Arthur Sullivan. This collaboration produced 14 operettas, nearly all of which are frequently performed today.

A Failed Lawyer, a Successful Writer

William Schwenck Gilbert was born in London on November 18, 1836. He was the oldest of four children—and the only son—born to Anne and William Gilbert. His sisters were Jane, Maud, and Florence. His father had been a surgeon in the Royal Navy. Shortly before young William's birth, his father inherited a large sum of money. He quickly retired from the navy and spent most of the next decade traveling with his family in France and Italy. Little is known about Anne Gilbert.

Little is also known of William's upbringing. One incident that he often recounted in later life occurred when he was about three or four. The family was in Naples, Italy, at the time. The little boy was walking in the street with his nurse. Two men came up to them and explained that they had been sent to take the boy back to his father. The trusting nurse turned William over to them. That was a mistake. The two men were actually kidnappers who held the boy for ransom. William's father promptly paid the money, and William was returned unharmed.

When he was eight, William began attending school in Boulogne, France, where the family was living at the time. Two years later the family moved back to England and young William spent three years at Western Grammar School in Brompton. Then he entered Great Ealing School in London. He did well in his classes, especially in Latin and Greek.

But there was a much more important influence at work in his life. By then, he was accustomed to attending plays. His father had always been very interested in opera, and William probably picked up this interest at a young age. Playing with a toy theater was one of his favorite pastimes as a child. Eventually his interest became a passion. Historian Andrew Crowther writes, "He began to dream of making a career of the theatre. He tried to run away from home to become an actor; but the actor he ran away to, Charles Kean, happened to know Gilbert's father, so that project came to nothing. Still, Gilbert began to write plays, and he produced them at his school, with himself as director.

"Even now, while still a schoolboy, Gilbert's character was beginning to show itself pretty clearly. A dominating character rather than a popular one; perhaps something of a bully; but redeeming these faults an irrepressible creativity. He could be charming, but there was always a sense of something cold and unapproachable within him."[1]

He was also very touchy, ready to take offense at any insult, whether it was real or imaginary. These qualities probably came from his parents. They were both cold and distant from their children. They also didn't get along very well with each other and were finally divorced in 1876.

After leaving Great Ealing, William entered King's College, London, where he began to study law. Then the Crimean War, in which Britain, France and Turkey fought against Russia, broke out in 1854. William wanted to become an officer with the Royal Artillery so that he could fight in the war. But the war ended in 1856, long before he could complete the necessary studies to obtain a commission. He went back to King's College and earned his bachelor of arts degree in 1857. To earn enough money to continue his law studies, he began working as a clerk in a local education department, a position he hated. He finally became an attorney in 1863, but he wasn't very successful. He had only a few clients.

By then, he had begun to write. His first several plays were rejected. Then he became a regular contributor to a magazine called *Fun*. He wrote many types of articles, including short stories, reviews of theater productions, and essays. He became best known for his "Bab Ballads," a series of humorous poems. They were very popular. Many people read them aloud at parties and other social gatherings. He also made frequent trips to Paris to attend operas there.

His first published play was *Dulcamara, or the Little Duck and the Great Quack,* which premiered late in 1866. *Dulcamara* was a comedy based on an opera by Gaetano Donizetti called *The Elixir of Love.* Its success gave him the confidence to propose to a woman named Lucy Turner, and they were married the following year. As was the case with his mother, very little is known about Lucy. Most people believe that the couple was happy during their long marriage. They never had any children.

Gilbert followed *Dulcamara* with four more comedies that were also based on popular operas. He wrote several other types of plays, and soon was turning out three or four every year. He also began to direct some of them. By 1870, he was so busy and so successful that he gave up his job with *Fun,* which hadn't paid very much money. The following year he was even busier. He wrote no fewer than seven plays. While it didn't attract much attention at the time, one of them was very significant. Called *Thespis,* it marked the first time that he worked with a young composer named Arthur Sullivan.

Arthur Conan Doyle

Arthur Conan Doyle

Like William S. Gilbert, Arthur Conan Doyle became a writer after starting his professional career in another field. Born on May 22, 1859, in Edinburgh, Scotland, Doyle became a physician and started a medical practice. In 1887, he published *A Study in Scarlet,* which introduced the world's most famous fictional detective, Sherlock Holmes, and his assistant, Dr. Watson.

A Study in Scarlet was very successful. Doyle followed it with *The Sign of Four* in 1890. Then he decided to specialize in ophthalmology, the study of the eye. He had very few patients. With time on his hands, he began writing short stories featuring Holmes and Watson. These were published in *The Strand* magazine.

One of Doyle's instructors in medical school had been Dr. Joseph Bell, who used careful observations to make deductions that led to his diagnoses. Years later, Sherlock Holmes used the same methods to solve crimes that completely baffled everyone else, including the police and Dr. Watson. "Elementary, my dear Watson," Holmes would often say when he wrapped up a case. It became one of the most famous phrases in the English language.

Eventually Doyle decided to kill off Holmes so that he could concentrate on "serious writing." In the story "The Final Problem," Holmes apparently falls off a cliff. The outcry was immediate. Thousands of people canceled their subscriptions to *The Strand.*

Several years later, Doyle bowed to popular demand and brought Holmes back in a prequel called *The Hound of the Baskervilles.* Then he resumed writing Sherlock Holmes short stories. In the first of these, the detective explains his reappearance to a startled Watson. He hadn't actually fallen off the cliff. He had remained hidden because he wanted criminals to believe that he was dead. That way he could fight crime from the shadows. Once he was back, more than 30 stories followed. The last one appeared in 1927.

Doyle also published numerous other works during this time. In his later life, he became passionate about spiritualism. He died in 1930.

Arthur Sullivan appears in a photograph taken relatively early in his life. He had become famous as a composer by the time he was 20.

CHAPTER 3

A Brilliant Young Composer

Arthur Seymour Sullivan was born in London on May 13, 1842, to Mary and Thomas Sullivan. Arthur was the couple's second and final child. He joined Frederick, who had been born in 1839. Arthur's father, Thomas, had been involved in music from the time he was a teenager, joining the band at the Royal Military College when he was 15.

At some point before the birth of his sons, Thomas resigned from the military band and tried to make a living playing in theater orchestras in London. He also gave lessons and copied music. He didn't earn much money, so the family lived close to poverty. In 1845 Thomas returned to the army and became sergeant bandmaster at the Royal Military College. That eased the family's financial situation. They could even afford a piano.

Not surprisingly, Arthur became interested in music at a young age. By the time he was eight, he had learned to play every wind instrument in addition to playing the piano at home. He also began to sing. About the same time, he composed his first work, a song called "By the Waters of Babylon." When he was nine, he began attending a private school in London. Three years later, he was admitted to the Chapel Royal, a highly selective institution that trained singers in addition to providing them with room and board. He quickly rose to the position of "first boy," the best singer in the school's chorus.

In 1856, Arthur was one of 17 young musicians who entered the competition to become the first recipient of the Mendelssohn Scholarship. Named for famous German composer Felix Mendelssohn, the scholarship allowed the winner to attend the Royal Academy of Music in London. That was England's best and most prestigious music school. At the age of 14, Arthur was the youngest entrant. He tied for first with the oldest, who was four years older than Arthur. They went head-to-head in a second round, and officials announced that the winner would receive a letter the following day. More than 40 years later, Arthur could vividly remember what happened.

"I spent the day in a fever of excitement," he wrote. "Every time I heard a knock at the door, my heart was in my mouth. The day wore on, but still no letter. Two o'clock came—three—four, I was beginning to lose hope. At last, rat-tat! The postman's knock. It was unmistakable. I crept into the hall. The maidservant passed by me, and went to the letter box. 'A letter for you, Master Sullivan,' she said. I took it from her, tore it open and then—I had won it. I don't think I ever felt such joy in my life."[1]

That was all he needed. The scholarship was originally for a period of one year. Arthur did so well that the committee renewed his scholarship for a second year. He continued to make excellent progress. The committee again renewed it. This time they added a bonus. They sent him to the Leipzig Conservatory

in Germany, an even better school than the Royal Academy. Fittingly, Mendelssohn himself had been the first director at the Leipzig Conservatory. While Arthur was initially sent there to study piano, he soon became more interested in conducting and composing. Arthur's professors were very impressed with his work. One of them even said that he was a better composer than the young German Johannes Brahms. That was especially high praise, because the professor was saying that an Englishman was superior to one of his own countrymen.

Arthur spent three years in Leipzig before returning to England. It didn't take him long to demonstrate what he had learned. In 1862, he wrote incidental music for a production of Shakespeare's play *The Tempest.* The response was immediate.

"At the conclusion there was a loud call for the composer who was greeted with the heartiest applause on all sides,"[2] wrote one reviewer. "Years on years have elapsed since we have heard a work by so young an artist so full of promise, so full of fancy,"[3] wrote another.

Some people even believed that the 20-year-old was already England's best composer. Unfortunately, not much money accompanied this glowing reputation. It was hard to make a living as a composer. As a result, Sullivan took on several other jobs during the next few years. He conducted orchestras as often as he could, played the organ, taught music students, and even served as a choir director.

Starting in 1865, he became romantically interested in a young woman named Rachel Scott Russell. Her wealthy family disapproved of him. They didn't believe that he would ever make enough money to support her at the level that they believed she

deserved. In addition, he was a musician, which was considered to be a low-class occupation. Soon they ordered Sullivan to stop seeing their daughter. The couple continued their romance in secret, but Rachel shared many of her parents' values. She was too practical to elope with a man who might not be able to provide her with enough financial support. Eventually they decided to stop seeing each other. After breaking up with Rachel, Arthur had relationships with several other women. None of them came close to marriage.

While he may have been unfortunate in love, his musical career was steadily moving forward. Much of the money in composing came from writing royalty ballads. These were popular songs in which the music publisher paid the composer a royalty based on sales. Sullivan wrote more than 100 of these. He wrote the music for church hymns, of which the most famous is "Onward, Christian Soldiers." He also composed a great deal of music for provincial music festivals.

In 1867, he composed the music for a small opera called *Cox and Box*. It was his first music for the theater, and he often said that that interest could be traced back to an 1862 meeting with noted operatic composer Gioachino Rossini. *Cox and Box* was also his most profitable composition. After this, he began looking around for other theatrical productions for which he could write. In 1871, he found one. ◆

The World's Biggest Ship

The Great Eastern

John Scott Russell, Rachel's father, was one of England's most important shipbuilders. In 1854, he and Isambard Kingdom Brunel designed the *Great Eastern*. Nearly 700 feet long and made of iron, it was the longest and heaviest ship that had ever been constructed. Launched in 1858, the ship was powered by steam engines that drove side paddle wheels and a propeller at the stern. There were also six masts, so the vessel could use wind power if the coal needed to produce steam ever ran out while she was still at sea.

The *Great Eastern* was designed to carry up to 4,000 passengers, but despite her great size she wasn't very comfortable. In addition, she was involved in two accidents during her ten voyages across the North Atlantic. Her owners lost a great deal of money. They sold her in 1864 to a company that wanted to lay telegraph cables across the North Atlantic. Her large size and ability to remain at sea for long periods made her ideal for that purpose. The following year, the *Great Eastern* had covered much of the distance from Great Britain to North America when the cable she was laying broke. The end couldn't be recovered, so the company tried again in 1866. This time they were successful. Messages that had previously taken weeks to send while ships crossed the Atlantic could now be conveyed in a few minutes. Over the next few years, the *Great Eastern* laid five more cables.

A French company bought the ship in 1874. They hoped to provide first-class passenger service between Europe and New York, but the venture soon fizzled out. The *Great Eastern* lay idle for more than a decade before being sold for scrap. The ship had been built so solidly that it took 200 men nearly two years to demolish her.

This is a view of the New Gaiety Theatre in London, which was built on the same site as the Old Gaiety Theatre. The Old Gaiety was the theater where Gilbert and Sullivan's first collaboration, Thespis, was performed in 1871.

A Fateful Meeting

By 1871, William Gilbert and Arthur Sullivan were well known in their respective fields—Gilbert in playwriting and Sullivan in composing. They were also somewhat familiar with each other's work.

Several years earlier, Gilbert had given Sullivan's music a favorable review in *Cox and Box*. "Mr. Sullivan's music is, in many places, of too high a class for the grotesquely absurd plot to which it is wedded,"[1] he commented.

While they probably met briefly for the first time in the summer of 1870, nothing came of it. Then in 1871, Gaiety Theatre manager John Hollingshead approached Sullivan. He was planning to produce a Christmas play called *Thespis*, written by Gilbert. No one knows why Hollingshead happened to unite the two men.

Thespis was reasonably successful, though the music has long since disappeared. This first collaboration didn't produce any sparks between the two men, and they promptly parted company. Sullivan continued to write music and Gilbert began rising to

prominence as a theater director; meanwhile he was still writing several plays every year.

"He kept at home a model theatre with striped wooden blocks for the performers," writes David Eden. "Using this he would work out all the stage directions for his play in advance, and arrive at the theatre with a perfectly clear picture in his own mind of what they should be. He would then proceed to drill the actors by rote until they conformed in every way with his wishes in the matter of stage position, gesture, and inflexion of voice. Since he could also design the scenery and costumes, the result was a kind of total theatre, in which every part faithfully reflected the dramatist's intentions and personality."[2]

With continuing success in their respective fields, neither man seemed to feel much of a need to work together again. It took a third man to reunite them. This was Richard D'Oyly Carte, the manager of the Royal Theatre. An ambitious man, he wanted to establish English comic opera. The French were already successful in this area, and he wanted to be able to compete with them. He had been impressed by *Thespis* when he saw it. Much more than either Gilbert or Sullivan, he thought that the two men might have a future together.

This future became the present early in 1875. D'Oyly Carte needed a one-act entertainment to accompany his production of an opera by Jacques Offenbach called *La Périchole*. First he approached Gilbert, who had already written a short skit called *Trial by Jury*. It was about a woman seeking monetary damages from a man who had broken off an engagement to her. D'Oyly Carte liked it. Then he suggested Sullivan as the composer. Soon afterward, Gilbert visited the other man and read his script aloud.

"'[Gilbert] read it through,' Sullivan recalled, 'as it seemed to me, in a perturbed sort of way, with a gradual crescendo of indignation, in the manner of a man considerably disappointed with what he had written. As soon as he had come to the last word he closed up the manuscript violently, apparently unconscious of the fact that he had achieved his purpose as far as I was concerned, inasmuch as I was screaming with laughter the whole time. The music was written, and the rehearsals completed, within the space of three weeks' time.'"3

Audiences shared Sullivan's reaction. He and Gilbert now realized that their collaboration might be fruitful. They began circulating their terms among London theater managers. Carte also realized that he'd stumbled onto something. He secured the backing of several wealthy investors and formed the Comedy Opera Company to produce new works by Gilbert and Sullivan. Their first production was *The Sorcerer,* which opened in 1877. It was reasonably successful, running for nearly 200 performances.

Then came *H.M.S. Pinafore.* After a slow start because of a heat wave in the summer of 1878, it soon attracted turnaway crowds. The following year, the comic opera onstage soon became a comic opera offstage as well. By this time, there was a lot of friction between Carte and his investors. He obtained legal control of the rights to *Pinafore* at the end of July 1879. Just before that date, the investors sent a band of men into the theater in an effort to gain control of the scenery and costumes so that they could open their own production. A fistfight broke out, and the audience could clearly hear the sound of the scuffle. After it died down, Carte transferred the show to another theater, where it continued to run for a total of more than 700 performances.

Gilbert, Sullivan, and D'Oyly Carte decided that they didn't need outside backers anymore. They agreed to form a three-man

partnership. They also decided that they would need a new show to take *Pinafore*'s place. Soon Gilbert and Sullivan began working on *The Pirates of Penzance,* which would open simultaneously in England and in the United States. Then they sailed for America.

By then the first signs of strain in the collaboration were beginning to appear. After their arrival in New York, the always-sensitive Gilbert felt that Sullivan was receiving more honors than he was. He began cracking jokes that made fun of his partner. There was also another strain. Just before leaving for the United States, Sullivan underwent a painful operation to remove kidney stones. Kidney problems would plague him for the rest of his life.

Pirates was just as much of a hit as *Pinafore.* It proved that the collaboration of the two men was not just a flash in the pan.

Several years later Gilbert described their working method. "I suppose we do it pretty much as any other two persons would who collaborate. In the first place, we arrange a meeting and I propose a subject, which, if entertained at all, is freely and fully discussed in all its bearings. Assuming that the broader lines of the plot have been thus settled, I write a scenario of fairish length—say twenty-six to thirty pages of foolscap [a type of cheap paper]—and this is subjected in its turn to a fresh discussion, and as a consequence, a second, third, or even fourth version of the scenario may be rendered necessary. Those passages and situations Sir Arthur thinks unsuitable to musical treatment I either modify or perhaps eliminate altogether. If I find that his difficulties or objections in any way knock the keystone out of my plan I tell him so, and he in turn yields a point or two.

"By this mode of procedure it will be readily perceived that there is some degree of give and take. Before a final plan is de-

cided upon, we may meet several times and gradually remove such obstacles as are likely to cause any hitch in the future harmonious blending of the dialogue and music."[4]

He also described some of their ground rules: "Sullivan and I resolved that our plots, however ridiculous, should be coherent; that our dialogue should be void of offence; that, on artistic principles, no man should play a woman's part and no woman a man's. Finally, we agreed that no lady of the company should be required to wear a dress that she could not wear with absolute propriety at a private fancy-dress ball."[5]

Many of the plots do seem ridiculous. For example, most of the action in *Pinafore* revolves around the forbidden love that a common seaman—Ralph Rakestraw—has for his captain's daughter, Josephine. Because of their differences in social status, they cannot be together. When Ralph tells her that he loves her, she replies, "Go, sir, and learn to cast your eyes on some village maiden in your own poor rank—they should be lowered before your captain's daughter."[6] Yet moments later she sings to herself, "I'd laugh my rank to scorn/In Union holy,/Were he more highly born/Or I more lowly."[7] Near the end of the operetta, it is revealed that Ralph and the captain were switched at birth. Ralph suddenly becomes the captain and the captain is now a common seaman. Now Ralph can marry the (former) captain's daughter.

The absurd plot hardly seemed to matter to enthusiastic audiences—then or now. People loved Sullivan's music. It was a perfect complement to Gilbert's words, which often made fun of Victorian-era conventions and well-known people. Because of his unhappy experiences as a lawyer, Gilbert especially liked to poke fun at the legal profession.

Their next collaboration was *Patience,* which opened in 1881. It was notable for being transferred a few months later to the new Savoy Theatre. D'Oyly Carte designed and built the Savoy to provide a permanent home for Gilbert and Sullivan operettas. It was the finest theater in London, the first to be entirely lit by electricity. It was also designed to provide for the safety of its audiences in the case of fire or other emergencies.

Each new production ran for many months after it opened. During each run, the two men had plenty of time to work on other projects.

Iolanthe and *Princess Ida,* the next two works, weren't quite as popular as their predecessors but still did well at the box office. By this time, Sullivan was in considerable pain due to his kidney problems. He was also beginning to tire of comic opera. His feelings were influenced by the knighthood he received from Queen Victoria in 1883. Now that he was Sir Arthur Sullivan, many critics and Sullivan himself felt that he should stop being frivolous and write only serious music. In 1884, he told his partners that he was finished writing operettas for the Savoy Theatre.

D'Oyly Carte decided to play hardball. The year before, Sullivan had signed a contract binding him to supply D'Oyly Carte with new operas for the next five years. The impresario demanded that the composer honor the contract.

That set up the first major conflict between Sullivan and his collaborator. Gilbert submitted a story he called "The Lozenge Plot" to Sullivan. The composer hated it. He refused to set it to music. Gilbert was a stubborn man. He thought that his play was just fine. He refused to offer anything else to Sullivan. Then one day he noticed a Japanese sword hanging on the wall in one of his rooms. That gave him the idea for an operetta set in Japan. It would become their single most famous work, *The Mikado.*

Richard D'Oyly Carte

D'Oyly Carte

While Richard D'Oyly Carte grew up with a musical background and was a composer, he is most famous for bringing Gilbert and Sullivan together. He also built the theaters in which many of their works were performed and acted as a mediator during their frequent quarrels.

Born on May 3, 1844, D'Oyly Carte attended the University School of London but dropped out to become more involved in his father's musical instrument company. After composing the music for several comic operas, he became interested in theatrical management and promotion. He was appointed business manager of the Royalty Theatre in 1874. Soon afterward he cemented his collaboration with his two soon-to-be famous partners.

In 1881 he built the Savoy Theatre to stage Gilbert and Sullivan productions. It was the first theater to be lit by electricity. Since electricity was still very new, many people were afraid of it. To prove how safe it was, D'Oyly Carte came on stage with a lighted bulb on the night the theater opened. He smashed the bulb with a hammer. When nothing happened to him, the audience was relieved. They applauded him for his "courage." Using electricity in the theater had several advantages. It became possible to gradually raise and lower the amount of illumination onstage and in the seating area. It was also more comfortable for audiences than gas lighting because it gave off less heat.

Soon afterward, D'Oyly Carte built the luxurious Savoy Hotel next to the theater. It was England's most modern hotel when it opened in 1889. It had innovations such as the first elevators in London, complete fireproofing throughout the structure, and 70 bathrooms.

D'Oyly Carte died in 1901, a few months after Sullivan. Today, people who attend, produce, or perform in Gilbert and Sullivan operas are known as Savoyards, after the theater that Richard D'Oyly Carte built to house their great collaboration.

This is the cover of the program given to patrons of The Mikado, which premiered in 1885. Considered as the finest product of the collaboration between Gilbert and Sullivan, the operetta was subtitled "The Town of Titipu" and took advantage of the era's fascination with Japanese culture.

CHAPTER 5

Cracks in the Foundation

The Mikado opened in March 1885. The premiere was well timed.

"The choice of a Japanese setting was a falling-in with the most popular artistic influence of the second half of the nineteenth century," writes Alan Jefferson. "From the fifties onwards there had been Japanese exhibitions, an enormous import of Japanese goods, and the leading artists and craftsmen all drew on the Japanese style. In a vein of the lightest humor Gilbert describes tortures, executions, corrupt officials . . . bowing and scraping, the sun and moon, suicide, volcanoes."[1]

Though it sounds rather grim, the subject inspired some of Gilbert's best and funniest lines. Sullivan wrote equally outstanding music. The result was that *The Mikado* ran for so long that both men had even more time than usual to work on their other projects. They finally resumed working together a year and a half later, on *Ruddigore*. When it opened, the two men heard something new: boos. Many people didn't like the new operetta. It ran for less than a year. By their previous standards, it was practically a failure.

Again they came to an impasse. They needed a new show, and Gilbert resubmitted his "Lozenge Plot." Sullivan didn't like it any better the second time around. Again Gilbert became stubborn. And again something on a wall saved the day. This time it was an advertisement for Tower Furnishing Company. The company was named after the famous Tower of London, and the illustration showed a yeoman warder, or guard. Nicknamed "beefeaters," these guards, in their bright red uniforms with gold trim, are still a primary tourist attraction at the Tower of London. Gilbert believed that an operetta set at the Tower of London could be successful. Sullivan agreed, and *The Yeomen of the Guard* opened in the fall of 1888. The two men were pleased with the result, considering it one of their finest works.

By this time, Sullivan was eager to start doing other work. "I have lost the liking for writing comic opera, and entertain very grave doubts as to my power of doing it," he wrote to Gilbert. "I have lost the necessary nerve for it, and it is not too much to say that it is distasteful to me."[2]

Despite the differences between Gilbert and Sullivan and the strain on their relationship, they renewed their partnership in 1889. *The Gondoliers* opened late that year. Set in Venice, Italy, it was destined to be their last great success. After it opened, Gilbert traveled to India for several months. When he returned, he received his first royalty check from *The Gondoliers*. It wasn't as large as he had expected. He asked why. Without his knowledge, D'Oyly Carte had spent a large sum of money redecorating part of the Savoy Theatre. Gilbert was outraged. He thought that D'Oyly Carte had spent far too much money, especially on the

carpet. He didn't think that the extra expense should have come out of his share. He went to Sullivan, asking for his partner's support in the argument, which by then had become known as the Carpet Quarrel. When Sullivan asked for a cooling-off period, Gilbert went ballistic. He interpreted the request as meaning that Sullivan was on D'Oyly Carte's side. On May 5, 1890, Gilbert wrote to Sullivan, "The time for putting an end to our collaboration has at last arrived."[3]

Gilbert took D'Oyly Carte to court. Sullivan testified in D'Oyly Carte's favor. The proceedings soon became rather nasty, which naturally led to ill feelings among the three men. Gilbert and Sullivan were reconciled in October the following year. In the meantime, they had again resumed their separate careers. For Sullivan, this finally took the form of a serious opera, *Ivanhoe*. It was an important part of another of D'Oyly Carte's plans. He had a radical new idea: presenting operas in English. Virtually every opera at that time was written and performed in its original language, usually Italian, German, or French. To accommodate the English operas, he built another new theater, the Royal English Opera House.

Ivanhoe was its initial production. It got off to a good start. "The first night, on 31 January 1891, was undoubtedly the climax of Sullivan's career: the military bandmaster's son conducted, in an opera house specially built for the purpose, the *magnum opus* [greatest work] which was to set English music on a new course of prosperity. For that night at least, *Ivanhoe* was the still point of the turning world. Few artists can have experienced such a moment, and in Sullivan's case it was entirely self-generated."[4]

Unfortunately, *Ivanhoe*'s success was only temporary. The new opera didn't last long enough for D'Oyly Carte to find anything

else to replace it. He soon had to sell the theater. One of the future owners would be Andrew Lloyd Webber, the composer of *Jesus Christ Superstar* and *Joseph and the Amazing Technicolor Dreamcoat.*

For Sullivan, there was no place to produce the future operas he wanted to compose. He also felt that he had to help D'Oyly Carte keep the Savoy Theatre open. That meant working again with Gilbert.

He almost didn't get the chance. He suffered yet another kidney attack. Only the action of putting him in a hot bath saved his life. When he recovered, he and Gilbert produced *Utopia, Limited,* which opened in 1893. It began as strongly as *The Mikado,* but it soon became apparent that it wasn't as good as the others. Attendance fell off sharply, which put the Savoy Theatre at risk again. Grudgingly, Sullivan realized that he had to work with Gilbert one final time. After several disagreements, the two men finally started working on *The Grand Duke.* It was their final collaboration, and perhaps their worst. It folded just four months after its opening in 1896.

Both men continued to work with other collaborators. But nothing was anywhere near as inspired as what they had produced during their first 12 years together.

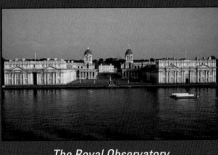

FYInfo

Setting Standards

The Royal Observatory

As the 19th century drew toward a close, there were many advances in communications and transportation. It became important to establish a single standard of time and space measurement to coordinate increasingly complicated schedules.

In 1884, the United States summoned 24 other nations to the International Meridian Conference. The Conference agreed on several principles. The most important was fixing the location of the prime meridian, or 0 degrees longitude. Longitude lines, also known as meridians, are the imaginary vertical lines that stretch from the North Pole to the South Pole. Unlike latitude, the horizontal lines that start at the equator and mark off parallel sections to the North and South Poles, there is no obvious starting point for longitude. In past years, sites ranging from Jerusalem to Paris had been used as the prime meridian.

The conference chose the meridian that runs through the Royal Observatory in Greenwich, England, just outside London, as the new starting point. Proceeding from Greenwich, everything is measured as either east or west longitude. They meet on the opposite side of the world from Greenwich, the International Date Line. If you cross that line from west to east, you gain a day. You lose a day if you go in the opposite direction. That is what enabled Phineas Fogg to win his wager in Jules Verne's novel *Around the World in 80 Days.* The book has been made into a movie several times, the most recent in 2004.

There were two major reasons for choosing Greenwich. One was that the United States and several other developed countries were already using Greenwich as the prime meridian. The other was England's dominance of the seas. Nearly three-fourths of existing nautical charts showed Greenwich as 0 degrees longitude.

Once Greenwich had been selected, time could be standardized. When it is noon in Greenwich, it is 7:00 A.M. on the east coast of the United States, 4:00 A.M. on the west coast, and midnight on the International Date Line.

A portrait of William S. Gilbert looks over part of the Savoy Theatre. Built in 1881, the theater was re-designed in 1929 by Basil Ionides. It now features Art Deco decoration and three seating levels.

CHAPTER 6

The End of the Music

The Savoy clung to life with a series of revivals. One of these, which included both the *Sorcerer* and *Trial by Jury*, marked the final public onstage meeting of Gilbert and Sullivan. It was September 1898.

"They took their call from opposite sides of the stage, with Carte between them, and walked off," writes Alan Jefferson. "There were no handshakes, and Gilbert ignored Sullivan."[1]

Though their disagreements mellowed during the next two years, the great partnership was over. As Gayden Wren says. "In retrospect, it's less surprising that Gilbert & Sullivan wrote nothing more after 1896 than that they worked together for as long as they did. Theatrical history offers no comparable example of such independently successful artists collaborating for so long. Each man brought his own star to the partnership; that it lasted so long is little short of miraculous."[2]

By this time, it was becoming increasingly evident to Sullivan that he would soon die. Time was short. He decided that in order

to write the great music that he still wanted to, he needed the support of a woman. At the age of 56, he proposed to 21-year-old Violet Beddington. She turned him down. He wrote several operas, but they didn't do well. His final work was the *Te Deum* in July 1900. Soon his ongoing kidney problems were aggravated by a sore throat and bronchitis. He suffered a fatal heart attack on the morning of November 22. The date was especially ironic, for it was the feast day of St. Cecilia, the patron saint of music.

"The combination of fame and financial success that his work achieved made Sir Arthur Sullivan an unhappy man," write Dorothy and Joseph Samachson. "Till the day of his death, he was embittered by the realization that the tuneful and unpretentious music he turned out for one operetta after another pleased millions of people, while the serious music he wrote with great effort apparently pleased no one, especially the critics."[3]

Gilbert would outlive his former partner by more than a decade. In 1890, he had moved to a large country estate called Grim's Dyke. It became somewhat of an animal sanctuary, with cats, dogs, deer, and monkeys roaming the grounds. He enjoyed hosting a wide variety of parties and also became interested in astronomy, photography, and magic.

In 1900 he took a long tour to Europe and the Mediterranean. He visited the Crimea area of Russia, where he had wanted to go as a soldier more than 40 years earlier. He was in Egypt when he heard of Sullivan's death. He was saddened by the news.

Richard D'Oyly Carte's widow, Helen, took over management of the Savoy Theatre. In 1906 she began mounting revivals of Gilbert and Sullivan operas. It marked the first awareness that Gilbert and Sullivan had produced something that could endure, that their collaboration had resulted in works of art rather than

temporary amusements. Despite this evidence that his name might live on in music history, Gilbert was furious. He disapproved of the productions because they emphasized singing rather than acting. The following year, he was finally knighted, nearly a quarter of a century after Sullivan had received the same honor. In 1909, he wrote his final libretto. It was for an opera entitled *Fallen Fairies.* The title seemed appropriate, because the opera failed.

Early in 1910, he wrote a short play called *The Hooligan,* which deals with the last moments of a condemned man. In an ironic twist, the man is reprieved—and promptly dies of a heart attack. The play premiered in 1911 and was very successful—and it soon held yet another ironic twist, this time in real life.

On the afternoon of May 29, 1911, Gilbert went to the lake at Grim's Dyke with two young women to give them swimming lessons. In their eagerness, the women went into the water before their host. One of them got into trouble. Gilbert rushed into the water and swam rapidly toward her rescue. But his 78-year-old heart failed under the strain. He sank into the depths of the lake.

A similar fate has never befallen their collaboration. Hundreds of Gilbert and Sullivan societies all over the world perform *H.M.S. Pinafore, The Pirates of Penzance, The Mikado,* and their other works annually. Tickets usually sell out quickly.

Their legacy lives on in music history. Two very different men were able to work together to create a unique combination of words and music that has never been surpassed. ◈

Rodgers and Hammerstein

In the mid-20th century, Richard Rodgers and Oscar Hammerstein II were as well known and highly regarded as Gilbert and Sullivan had been several decades earlier.

Rodgers (left) and Hammerstein (right)

Hammerstein was born in 1895 into a theatrical family. He began studying law in college but quit to devote his time to writing plays and lyrics for musicals. Before he was 30, he worked with noted composers such as Sigmund Romberg and George Gershwin to revive the operetta, which had been in decline since Gilbert and Sullivan broke up. Then he collaborated with Jerome Kern on *Showboat,* which many people consider the finest American musical ever produced.

Born in 1902, Rodgers also achieved success while in his 20s. He collaborated with Lorenz Hart on a number of popular comedies set to music that became Broadway hits. The two men spent the early 1930s in Hollywood, then returned to Broadway, where such works as *On Your Toes, Babes in Arms,* and *Pal Joey* established their enduring fame. Behind the scenes, however, they were drifting apart. One factor was Hart's increasing ill health. When Hart died in 1943, Rodgers began his association with Hammerstein.

They made their mark immediately with *Oklahoma!,* which blended two forms—operetta and musical comedy—to become the first musical play. It was followed by *Carousel* (1945), *South Pacific* (1949), *The King and I* (1951), and several others. They also produced *State Fair* specifically for Hollywood. In 1959, their final collaboration was perhaps the 20th century's best-known musical, *The Sound of Music.* The 1965 film version with Julie Andrews remains very popular today.

Hammerstein died in 1960. Rodgers collaborated with several lyricists and remained active until shortly before his death in 1979. Proof of their enduring legacy came in 1996 when *State Fair* and *The King and I,* along with *Showboat,* enjoyed sold-out and award-winning Broadway revivals. Another legacy is their 15 Academy Awards, 34 Tonys, and many other honors. In 1999 they were portrayed together on a postage stamp.

Chronology

William S. Gilbert

1836   Born on November 18 in London
1839   Kidnapped in Naples, Italy
1844   Attends school in Boulogne, France
1846   Enters Western Grammar School in Brompton, England
1849   Enters Great Ealing School
1857   Receives bachelor of arts degree from King's College, London
1861   Begins contributing to *Fun* magazine
1866   Writes *Dulcamara*
1867   Marries Lucy Turner on August 6
1871   Collaborates with Sullivan on *Thespis*
1875   *Trial by Jury* becomes first successful collaboration with Sullivan
1890   Moves to Grim's Dyke
1893   Appointed justice of the peace in Middlesex County
1907   Receives knighthood
1911   Dies in Grim's Dyke on May 29

Arthur Sullivan

1842   Born in London on May 13
1852   Becomes chorister in Her Majesty's Chapel Royal
1856   Wins Mendelssohn Scholarship at Royal Academy of Music
1862   Writes incidental music for Shakespeare's play *The Tempest*
1867   Composes music for *Cox and Box*
1871   Collaborates with Gilbert on *Thespis*
1879   Undergoes operation to remove kidney stones
1883   Receives knighthood from Queen Victoria
1884   Announces that he won't write any more operettas
1886   Composes cantata *The Golden Legend*
1891   *Ivanhoe* premieres
1900   Dies in London on November 22

In collaboration

1875   *Trial by Jury* becomes first major collaboration
1877   *The Sorcerer* premieres
1878   *H.M.S. Pinafore* premieres
1879   Form partnership with Richard D'Oyly Carte; travel to United States; *Pirates of Penzance* premieres in London and New York
1881   *Patience* premieres; Savoy Theatre opens in London
1884   First major disagreement
1885   *The Mikado* premieres
1889   *The Gondoliers,* their final successful collaboration, premieres
1890   "Carpet Quarrel" puts temporary end to partnership
1893   Partnership is revived with premiere of *Utopia, Limited*
1896   *Grand Duke* marks final collaboration

Timeline in History

1805   Royal Navy under the command of Admiral Horatio Nelson defeats combined French and Spanish fleet at the battle of Trafalgar.

1809   Composer Felix Mendelssohn is born.

1815   Napoléon is defeated at the battle of Waterloo and sent into exile.

1818   Mary Wollstonecraft Shelley writes *Frankenstein*.

1823   President James Monroe declares the Monroe Doctrine, which closes the American continent to further colonization by European countries.

1827   Composer Ludwig van Beethoven dies.

1832   Lewis Carroll, the author of *Alice's Adventures in Wonderland,* is born.

1836   Charles Dickens publishes *Pickwick Papers*.

1839   Industrialist and philanthropist John D. Rockefeller is born.

1845   The failure of the potato crop in Ireland leads to widespread famine.

1853   Henry Steinway and his three sons organize Steinway & Sons, one of the world's leading piano manufacturers.

1857   English composer Edward Elgar is born; his "Pomp and Circumstance" is often played at high school and college graduation ceremonies.

1864   "In God We Trust" appears for the first time on U.S. coins.

1874   British statesman Winston Churchill is born.

1877   Thomas Edison invents the phonograph.

1887   Sir Arthur Conan Doyle publishes *A Study in Scarlet,* the first Sherlock Holmes mystery.

1892   Peter Tchaikovsky's ballet *The Nutcracker* premieres in St. Petersburg, Russia.

1895   U.S. salesman King C. Gillette invents the safety razor.

1898   The United States defeats Spain in the Spanish-American War and becomes a world power.

1900   The cake walk becomes the most popular dance in the United States.

1906   Norwegian explorer Roald Amundsen determines the location of the magnetic North Pole, the direction toward which all compasses point.

1911   The *Mona Lisa,* Leonardo da Vinci's famous painting, is stolen from the Louvre in Paris; it is discovered two years later and returned.

1920   Women gain the right to vote in the United States.

1925   Tennessee schoolteacher John Scopes goes on trial for teaching the theory of evolution.

1927   Philo T. Farnsworth sends first television picture using electricity.

1933   Major League Baseball plays its first All-Star game.

1940   American composer Irving Berlin writes "White Christmas."

1943   Rodgers and Hammerstein's *Oklahoma!* premieres.

1947   Zip-A-Dee-Doo-Dah wins Academy Award for best song.

1956   Elvis Presley records "Heartbreak Hotel," his first record to go gold.

1964   The Beatles appear in the United States for the first time and transform rock music.

Chapter Notes

Chapter 1
Pirates and Pinafores

1. David Eden, *Gilbert & Sullivan: The Creative Conflict* (Cranbury, N.J.: Associated University Presses, 1986), pp. 24–25.
2. Harold Schonberg, *The Lives of the Great Composers* (New York: W.W. Norton, 1981), pp. 335–336.
3. Ibid., p. 335.
4. Arthur Jacobs, *Arthur Sullivan: A Victorian Musician* (New York: Oxford University Press), 1984, pp. 123–124.
5. Jefferson, Alan, *The Complete Gilbert & Sullivan Opera Guide* (New York: Facts on File, 1984), p. 83.

Chapter 2
A Failed Lawyer, a Successful Writer

1. Andrew Crowther, "W. S. Gilbert Society Homepage," (http://web.ukonline.co.uk/ajcrowth/wsgsoc.htm, August 13, 2003).

Chapter 3
A Brilliant Young Composer

1. Arthur Jacobs, *Arthur Sullivan: A Victorian Musician* (New York: Oxford University Press, 1984), p. 12.
2. Ibid., p. 27.
3. Ibid.

Chapter 4
A Fateful Meeting

1. David Eden, *Gilbert & Sullivan: The Creative Conflict* (Cranbury, N.J.: Associated University Presses, 1986), p. 19.
2. Ibid., p. 22.

3. Arthur Jacobs, *Arthur Sullivan: A Victorian Musician* (New York: Oxford University Press, 1984), p. 90.
4. Charles Hayter, *Gilbert and Sullivan* (London: MacMillan Publishers Ltd., 1987), pp. 21–22.
5. Jacobs, p. 69.
6. Alan Jefferson, *The Complete Gilbert & Sullivan Opera Guide* (New York: Facts on File, 1984), p. 83.
7. Ibid.

Chapter 5
Cracks in the Foundation

1. Alan Jefferson, *The Complete Gilbert & Sullivan Opera Guide* (New York: Facts on File, 1984), p. 184.
2. Charles Hayter, *Gilbert and Sullivan* (London: MacMillan Publishers Ltd., 1987), p. 19.
3. Ibid., p. 20.
4. David Eden, *Gilbert & Sullivan: The Creative Conflict* (Cranbury, N.J.: Associated University Presses, 1986), p. 36.

Chapter 6
The End of the Music

1. Alan Jefferson, *The Complete Gilbert & Sullivan Opera Guide* (New York: Facts on File, 1984), p. 20.
2. Gayden Wren, *A Most Ingenious Paradox: The Art of Gilbert & Sullivan* (New York: Oxford University Press, 2001), p. 277.
3. Dorothy Samachson and Joseph Samachson, *Masters of Music: Their Works, Their Lives, Their Times* (New York: Doubleday & Company, 1967), p. 235.

For Further Reading

For Young Adults

James, Alan, and Andrew Codd. *Gilbert and Sullivan: The Illustrated Lives of the Great Composers*. London: Omnibus Press, 1993.

Karr, Kathleen. *Gilbert and Sullivan: Set Me Free*. New York: Hyperion Books for Children, 2003.

Langstaff, John. *I Have a Song to Sing, O!: An Introduction to the Songs of Gilbert and Sullivan*. New York: Margaret K. McElderry, 1994.

Works Consulted

Ainger, Michael. *Gilbert and Sullivan: A Dual Biography*. New York: Oxford University Press, 2002.

Eden, David. *Gilbert & Sullivan: The Creative Conflict*. Cranbury, N.J.: Associated University Presses, 1986.

Hayter, Charles. *Gilbert and Sullivan*. London: MacMillan Publishers Ltd., 1987.

Jacobs, Arthur. *Arthur Sullivan: A Victorian Musician*. New York: Oxford University Press, 1984.

Jefferson, Alan. *The Complete Gilbert & Sullivan Opera Guide*. New York: Facts on File, 1984.

Pearson, Hesketh. *Gilbert: His Life and Strife*. New York: Harper & Brothers, 1957.

Samachson, Dorothy, and Joseph Samachson. *Masters of Music: Their Works, Their Lives, Their Times*. New York: Doubleday & Company, 1967.

Schonberg, Harold. *The Lives of the Great Composers*. New York: W.W. Norton, 1981.

Sutton, Max Keith. *W. S. Gilbert*. Boston: Twayne Publishers, 1975.

Wren, Gayden. *A Most Ingenious Paradox: The Art of Gilbert & Sullivan*. New York: Oxford University Press, 2001.

On the Internet

W. S. Gilbert Society
http://web.ukonline.co.uk/ajcrowth/wsgsoc.htm
The Gilbert and Sullivan Archive
http://diamond.boisestate.edu/gas/html
"The Life of W. S. Gilbert," by Andrew Crowther
http://diamond.boisestate.edu/gas/html/gilbert_l.html
"Sir Arthur Sullivan," by David Ewen
http://diamond.boisestate.edu/gas/html/sullivan2.html
Arthur Sullivan
http://www.fact-index.com/a/ar/arthur_sullivan.html
Sherlock Holmes on the Web
http://www.sherlockian.net/
Sidebar: The World's Biggest Ship
Ships of the World: An Historical Encyclopedia—"Great Eastern"
http://college.hmco.com/history/readerscomp/ships/html/
sh_040800_greateastern.htm

For Further Reading (Cont'd)

National Maritime Museum, Royal Observatory Greenwich: "The Great Eastern"
http://www.nmm.ac.uk/site/request/setTemplate:singlecontent/contentTypeA/
    conWebDoc/contentId/146
Sidebar: Richard D'Oyly Carte
"Richard D'Oyly Carte and the Dynasty He Founded," by Diana Burleigh
http://math.boisestate.edu/gas/html/carte_diana.html
Sidebar: Setting Standards
National Maritime Museum, Royal Observatory Greenwich: "The Prime Meridian at
    Greenwich"
www.nmm.ac.uk/site/request/setTemplate:singlecontent/ contentTypeA/conWebDoc/
    contentId/1343
"The International Meridian Conference"
http://millennium-dome.com/info/conference.htm
Sidebar: Rodgers and Hammerstein
American Masters, "Richard Rodgers"
http://www.pbs.org/wnet/americanmasters/database/rodgers_r.html
Rodgers and Hammerstein Organization: Biography, "Hammerstein, Oscar II"
http://www3.rnh.com/rhstein/bios/
    Show_bio.asp?Bio_Name1=Hammerstein,+Oscar+II&Flag=-1

Glossary

copyright (CAH-pee-rite)—the exclusive right to publish or perform a work of art.

opera (AH-p'rah)—a musical drama in which the actors sing the dialogue.

operetta (ah-per-EH-tuh)—a lighter form of opera, usually a comedy or romance.

royalty (ROY-uhl-tee)—a fee paid to authors and/or composers for the right to perform their work.

Selected Works

Trial by Jury	The Mikado
The Sorcerer	Ruddigore
H.M.S. Pinafore	The Yeomen of the Guard
The Pirates of Penzance	The Gondoliers
Patience	Utopia Limited
Iolanthe	The Grand Duke
Princess Ida	

Index

Beddington, Violet 40
Brunel, Isambard Kingdom 23
"Carpet Quarrel" 34-35
D'Oyly Carte, Helen 40
D'Oyly Carte, Richard 26, 27, 28, 31
Donizetti, Gaetano 15
Doyle, Arthur Conan 17
Gilbert and Sullivan, works of
    Gondoliers, The 34
    Grand Duke, The 36
    H.M.S Pinafore 7-10, 27, 28, 29,
      41
    Iolanthe 30
    Mikado, The 30, 33, 36, 41
    Patience 30
    Pirates of Penzance, The 10, 28, 41
    Princess Ida 30
    Ruddigore 33-34
    Sorcerer, The 27, 39
    Thespis 15, 25
    Trial by Jury 26, 39
    Utopia, Limited 36
    Yeomen of the Guard 34
Gilbert, Anne (mother) 13, 14
Gilbert, Florence (sister) 13
Gilbert, Jane (sister) 13
Gilbert, Lucy Turner (wife) 15
Gilbert, Maud (sister) 13
Gilbert, William (father) 13, 14
Gilbert, William S.
    Begins writing career 15
    Birth of 13
    Death of 41
    Disagreements with Sullivan 28, 30,
      32, 34-35
    Early interest in theater 14
    First collaboration with Sullivan 25
    Forms partnership with Sullivan and
      D'Oyly Carte 28
    Kidnapping of 13
    Last meeting with Sullivan 39
    Law studies of 14-15
    Marriage of 15
    Moves to Grim's Dyke 40
    Receives knighthood 41
    Working method with Sullivan 28-29

Works of
    Bab Ballads 15
    Dulcamara 15
    Fallen Fairies 41
    Hooligan, The 41
    Lozenge Plot 30, 34
Hollingshead, John 25
Holmes, Sherlock 17
Mendelssohn, Felix 20, 21
Napoleon 11
Napster 7
Nelson, Admiral Horatio 11
Offenbach, Jacques 26
Rossini, Gioachino 22
Russell, John Scott 23
Russell, Rachel Scott 21, 22, 23
Sousa, John Philip 8
Sullivan, Arthur S.
    Birth of 19
    Death of 40
    Disagreements with Gilbert 28, 30,
      32, 34-35
    Early interest in music 19
    First collaboration with Gilbert 25
    Forms partnership with Gilbert and
      D'Oyly Carte 28
    Health problems of 28, 30, 36, 39
    Knighted by Queen Victoria 30
    Last meeting with Gilbert 39
    Relationship with Rachel Scott
      Russell 21-22
    Wins Mendelssohn Scholarship 20
    Working method with Gilbert 28-9
    Works of
      By the Waters of Babylon 20
      Cox and Box 22, 25
      Ivanhoe 35
      Te Deum 40
      Tempest, The 21
Sullivan, Frederick (brother) 19
Sullivan, Mary (mother) 19
Sullivan, Thomas (father) 19
Verne, Jules 37
Watson, Dr. 17
Webber, Andrew Lloyd 36